NAVIGATING YOUR

NEW YORK DIVORCE AGREEMENT CASE:

Prenups, Separations, Settlements & Mediation

DAVID I. BLIVEN, ESQ.

Jacobs & Whitehall
9600 Escarpment Blvd
Suite 745-282
Austin, TX 78749
www.jacobsandwhitehall.com

Ordering Information:

Quantity sales. Special discounts are available on quantity purchases by corporations, associations, and others. For details, contact the publisher at the address above.

Orders by U.S. trade bookstores and wholesalers. Please contact Jacobs & Whitehall: Tel: (888) 570-7338 or visit www.jacobsandwhitehall.com.

Printed in the United States of America

Published in 2024

ISBN: 978-1-954506-99-2

PREFACE

More than 90% of divorce cases end in settlements[1] - indeed, in this author's experience, the percentage can range as high as 95-98%.

Furthermore, given the vastly increasing costs of divorce litigation, more people are executing prenuptial agreements than ever before. Indeed, one survey found the numbers increased from a mere 3% in 2010 to roughly 15% just 12 years later[2].

Likewise, an increasing percentage of people are opting to resolve their divorce & custody disputes via mediation - as opposed to costly litigation[3].

---

1 https://legal-info.lawyers.com/family-law/divorce/what-types-of-divorces-typically-go-to-trial.html.

2 https://www.npr.org/2023/08/30/1196872794/prenups-arent-just-for-the-rich-and-famous-heres-when-to-consider-one#:~:text=In%202022%2C%20the%20market%20research,a%20premarital%20or%20prenuptial%20agreement.

3 https://mediate.com/what-the-statistics-tell-us-about-divorce-and-custody-mediation/.

That said, there are very few books out there which give people the nuts-and-bolts of how to choose. What's involved in a prenuptial agreement? Why should I choose mediation versus litigation? And what do those terms ever mean?

Those questions - and similar ones - from potential clients are the reason I'm writing this book. This book is NOT a "do-it-yourself" guide. I still strongly recommend you retain an attorney to draft your prenuptial, separation or divorce agreement for you. At the least, if you choose to draft one yourself - or obtain one off the internet - you should consult a good matrimonial attorney, who can review what you drafted & advise you of its legality as well as items you may have missed. But ultimately, if the items you're addressing are worth preserving - kids, property and assets - then it's also worth retaining an attorney to make sure it's done right.

Additionally, at the end of this book is an addendum of worthy issues & questions you should consider in preparation for the agreement process. The questionnaire is NOT an exhaustive list - indeed, when I review this with potential clients or clients, I often deviate from this list. But it's a good starting point - completing it before you meet with the attorney will allow you to "hit the ground running" & will allow you to save time & money.

For assistance in finding a mediator near you, you can consult the NY State Council on Divorce Mediation website:

https://nyscdm.memberclicks.net/find-a-mediator#/

DISCLAIMER

This publication is intended to be used for educational purposes only. No legal advice is being given, and no attorney-client relationship is intended to be created by reading this material. The author assumes no liability for any errors or omissions or for how this book or its contents are used or interpreted, or for any consequences resulting directly or indirectly from the use of this book. For legal or any other advice, please consult an experienced attorney or the appropriate expert, who is aware of the specific facts of your case and is knowledgeable in the law in your jurisdiction.

The Law Offices of David Bliven

www.blivenlaw.net

White Plains Office
19 Court St.
Suite 206
White Plains, NY 10601
(914) 468-0968

Bronx Office
3190 Riverdale Avenue
Suite 1
Bronx, NY 10463
(718) 725-9600

TABLE OF CONTENTS

i. **Preface** **3**

1. **How To Prepare for An Impending Divorce In New York** **9**

2. **Understanding Divorce Settlements In New York** **28**

3. **Negotiating A Divorce Agreement In New York** **41**

4. **The Role of Parent Coordinators & Facilitators** **58**

5. **New York Family Law Mediation: The Basics Every Family Needs to Know** **72**

6. **Prenuptial & Postnuptial Agreements In New York** **94**

7. **Legal Separation Agreements In New York** **115**

ii. **About The Author** 140

iii. **Testimonials** 142

iv. **Index** 147

v. **Notes** 149

Chapter 1

How To Prepare for An Impending Divorce In New York

It's no secret that getting divorced is one of the most stressful events you can experience in life - in fact, it is frequently ranked as #2 on lists of life's most stressful experiences. While you may not be able to alleviate the stress of an impending divorce entirely, one way to decrease your stress when going through a divorce is to be prepared.

In this chapter, you can learn effective strategies to help you prepare in advance if you anticipate a divorce or separation in your future, including:

- How you can plan ahead financially for divorce and child support, and why you need to create a paper trail for child custody issues.
- Which professionals you should work with, in addition to your divorce lawyer, who can help you prepare for or get through your divorce.
- Why moving funds around before your divorce should not be part of your financial strategy.

If I Anticipate a Divorce, How Can I Prepare In Advance To Obtain The Best Outcome?

There are several things you should keep in mind if you are planning to file for divorce, or you believe your spouse may be planning to file for divorce. Proper planning when a divorce is anticipated will help you obtain the best possible outcome.

The first thing you should be aware of is your income in regard to future spousal support or child support. Under New York State law, the amount you will pay for alimony (spousal support or maintenance) or child support is a strict amount based on your income[4]. This amount will be calculated based on your most recently filed taxes.

Like many people, you may be currently working overtime, picking up extra shifts, or even working multiple jobs to bring in extra income for your family. However, it is worth noting that all of this extra income will count when it comes to calculating your alimony or child support costs.

If you think your spouse could potentially sue you for alimony or child support, you should consider your income - even if the divorce might not occur for another several months or a year. Earning extra income could lock you into a position where your spousal or child support payments are excessive or above what you can afford without working yourself into the ground.

---

4 https://ww2.nycourts.gov/divorce/MaintenanceChildSupportTools.shtml

It may be worth having a conversation with your spouse and communicating that, for your mental and physical health, you need to scale back. However, if you wait until divorce proceedings have been initiated, it will probably be too late to adjust your income for support payment calculations.

Second, if you anticipate child custody or visitation will be an issue, it is essential to begin gathering evidence to support your case well in advance. It is common in divorce trials for both parents to argue that they should have custody, without providing proof as to why they should have primary care of their children.

In these cases, it is your word against the other parent. How is the Judge supposed to know who is telling the truth without actual evidence?

One way to show proof is to create a paper trail, such as a shared calendar that tracks what tasks you or your spouse are doing for the child over several months. Electronic communication can also be helpful to track parenting responsibilities. For example, if you ask your spouse to take your child to a playdate or an appointment and they refuse, this can help provide evidence to the court[5].

Like with financial planning, it is important to begin gathering this evidence long before the divorce is filed. Ideally, if these issues may be contested, you should have some evidence gathered to support your case before you schedule a consultation with your divorce attorney.

What Professionals Can Help Me with My Divorce Case?

If you believe a divorce is in your future, you should, of course, work with a divorce attorney. But you should also consider working with a financial planner or an asset manager who is skilled in counseling clients for divorce cases.

---

[5] It is beyond the scope of this book to provide a comprehensive guide on preparing for a contested custody case. You should therefore consult my books "Navigating Your New York Family Court Case" or "Navigating Your New York Contested Divorce Case" & specifically review the chapters on custody.

If possible, you should work with a certified divorce financial planner (https://institutedfa.com/). These financial planners are trained to counsel people who are going through a divorce or will imminently be going through a divorce. They are certified by an independent organization to help you put your income, assets, and properties in the best position.

A certified divorce financial planner will help you obtain a good outcome, and can also provide you with a realistic outlook of your situation. They can also work with your divorce attorney to improve your case. Another professional to consider is an accountant who has handled cases involving divorcing couples.

If child custody may be an issue, work with a forensic psychologist, domestic violence advocate or substance abuse counselor if those maybe issues in your case. You may also consider retaining a private investigator.

You should meet with professionals as early as possible if you think there may be contested issues, such as assets, property, alimony, or child support. It often takes months to get your finances sorted, and if you wait until the divorce is being filed, it is usually too late.

Do I Need to Work with A Financial Advisor Before Filing For Divorce?

Whether or not you need to work with a financial advisor before your divorce depends on what financial issues might be contested in the divorce. If you have no money, assets, or property, you likely do not need to see a financial planner.

However, if there will be contested issues of assets, property division, alimony (or spousal maintenance), or child support, then we recommend that you work with a financial planner. A certified divorce financial planner can be an enormous asset to you during a divorce, as their job is to put you in the best financial position possible.

It is relatively inexpensive to schedule an appointment or consultation, or even several consultations, with a financial planner. And if the money at stake is hundreds of thousands or millions of dollars, then spending a few hundred dollars on sessions with a certified divorce financial planner is well worth it.

Many people think just hiring a divorce attorney is good enough. But it is not good enough in some cases, especially if you have a high income or high net worth case. When there are contested financial issues, it is crucial to also work with a certified divorce financial planner (at the least) or forensic accountant.

If everything is black and white and the financial stakes are lower, you may not need a financial planner. However, you should schedule a consultation with your divorce attorney as soon as possible so your divorce attorney can inform you on whether you should also consult with a financial planner.

If I Want to Start Building My Financial Future Without My Spouse, Can I Move Funds to Other Bank Accounts or Give Them To Someone I Trust?

In most divorce cases, there is a lookback period of three years. Moving assets around from one account to another or giving them to a family member may not help you in your divorce case. Indeed, in New York State, there is an automatic order prohibiting you from moving your funds to other accounts[6] after the case is filed.

Even if you move funds a year before filing for your divorce, you still have to submit a net worth statement listing all of your assets. This includes your bank account records, investment accounts, retirement accounts, and more. You must submit updated records on the date of filing, but you may have to show the last three years of records. In some cases, the court or opposing counsel can look at records from even earlier.

Can I Protect Myself from My Spouse's Debts Or Ensure My Spouse Will Help Me Pay The Debts We Incurred Together?

In a New York divorce, the presumptive rule is that marital debts are divisible 50-50, as of the time of

---

[6] Except as one has commonly done. Even so, there is a strict prohibition on moving funds from retirement accounts.

the filing. Under New York state law, names on accounts do not matter, which means that both parties generally share debt equally.

The only factor which matters (in terms of whether it is marital debt) is whether the debt was accrued during the time of the marriage. If it did, then the debt is *presumptively* divisible 50-50. However, there may be ways to avoid paying for high debts incurred solely by your spouse, and you should have a lawyer look into certain debt circumstances.

For example, imagine your spouse informs you they have $30,000 on their credit card. You did not know anything about this debt, and you do not understand how it occurred since there is enough money for both of you to pay your expenses. In this case, you would want to communicate with your spouse and investigate how and when this debt occurred.

The best method for resolving this is to have a paper trail. You could do this by asking for credit card statements or account access. You may also want to work with a financial planner who can help you both look over the records and create a plan to pay off the debt.

Ideally, you want to find out *how the debt accrued.* In other words, did your spouse start purchasing many expensive clothes for themselves, contrary to their ordinary behavior? While this is not always the case, it can be common for one spouse to hide money or debt when anticipating a divorce.

One technique you can use when reviewing debt statements is to check if there are high charges from particular stores. Your divorce attorney would want to look over receipts, invoices, and bills for specific purchases. Depending on the amount of debt, this can help determine whether it is worth sending a subpoena to the store where your spouse purchased items.

A subpoena can show whether a particular item was returned. Sometimes individuals purchase high-value items and then return them to get cash rather than putting the money back on the credit card. They can then hide the cash or give it to a friend or family member to keep for them.

For example, if your combined credit card debt is $30,000 - and because it is presumptively divisible 50-50 - you now presumptively owe your spouse $15,000. An unwitting spouse might agree to pay for half of the debt, not knowing the full situation. This is just one of several situations you may want a professional to investigate, especially if there are suspicious charges on the debt statements.

Do I Need to Move Out Before My Divorce Is Final? Will Moving Out Revoke My Property Rights?

In general, you do not need to move out before your divorce is finalized, nor does this negate any of your property rights. Parties are not obligated to remain living under the same roof, but one should consider a few factors before moving out.

For starters, you and your spouse should have an agreement about who will pay the rent, mortgage, or utility bills for the property while the divorce is pending. You should ensure there is confirmation or a stipulation in place to determine who is responsible for paying each bill.

You probably would not want to begin renting another residence if you still owe half of the mortgage on the shared property. Before you sign a lease on an apartment or another house, you should make sure you can afford both payments.

In addition, if there are any spousal maintenance or child support issues, you should confirm those issues before you move out. At the least, you should get a stipulation through your divorce attorney.

In a recent case, a client signed a lease on an apartment, but the management office informed her that after running her credit check, they did not believe she could afford the apartment. They asked for either a co-signer for the lease or a certification from a divorce attorney stating what she was expected to receive from her divorce case.

These types of situations can cause many problems, especially if you have already made plans to move, rented a moving truck, paid application fees, etc. Before deciding to move out or sign another lease, you should make sure to confirm any potential issues.

Will The Court Order Me or My Spouse To Pay Child Support From The Time Of Separation?

Usually, child support is paid starting from the date of the divorce filing and is not paid retroactively to the date of separation. If you and your spouse are separating, or if you anticipate a divorce in the future, it is crucial to communicate with your spouse and figure out child support sooner rather than later. This is especially true if one parent is a stay-at-home parent, or if one of you moves out.

If your spouse does not want to commit to child support payments or does not follow through on their commitment, you should file for divorce, or possibly even file an emergency motion. The courts generally respond quickly to emergency motions, and you will often get a court date in as soon as two to four weeks. Even in the greater New York City area, they should see you within a month or so.

How Important Is It to Meet With An Attorney Before I Decide To Get Divorced?

The divorce process is stressful, and trying to understand the timing of when you should take certain steps is not always clear. Whether or not you should meet with an attorney before you decide to get divorced depends on the specifics of your situation.

For some couples, it is fine to meet with an attorney once they have decided to get divorced and they are ready to file. However, in some cases, damage has already been done before you meet with an attorney to file for your divorce.

Our firm has many real-world examples of the damage that can occur if you decide to wait to speak with an attorney…

Example #1: Losing Money

One of our clients consulted our firm on a divorce matter after he and his wife had just sold a co-op and received $250,000 in equity. We suggested that if they wanted to terminate the marriage, it would be best not to wait to file the divorce. Unfortunately, this client did not take our advice and waited for nearly two years before he decided to take action.

When you file for divorce in the state of New York, it places automatic orders on your accounts so neither party can close or transfer money out of accounts, except in the usual course of business (https://www.nycourts.gov/LegacyPDFS/divorce/forms_instructions/Notice.pdf). When this client finally hired our firm, he informed us the equity he and his wife received had been in the joint account. However, his wife had taken the entire $250,000 and placed it in her own account, leaving him with nothing.

His case had already been damaged before it even started. When we spoke to the Divorce Judge, he agreed it was a good argument for trial - but did not order our client's wife to restore or split the funds she had taken.

Our client's wife then had $250,000 to spend on divorce lawyers, while he had nothing to spend on an attorney. Her divorce attorney used the money to their advantage. Eventually, our client had to agree to a settlement vastly lower than what he would have received if he had been able to continue to retain an attorney.

Example #2: Self-Sabotaging Behavior

Before working with us, another client made threats and accusations toward his soon-to-be ex-wife, including death threats - which she reported. He tried to explain during the divorce case that he didn't mean it literally – it was just his morbid sense of humor. He also explained he was going through extreme depression and admitted it had been wrong to joke in that way.

However, his wife had evidence with audio transcriptions, and she requested an order of protection and supervised visits for their children. The Judge granted her request immediately, putting our client at a vast disadvantage in any custody or access litigation.

Example #3: Lack of Evidence

Divorce cases are often closely linked with child custody cases. One of our clients had decided to represent herself in her child custody case before eventually retaining our firm to represent her. During that time, she made allegations of child abuse regarding the child's other parent. She filed a petition to modify the child custody settlement that had been arranged a month before.

However, the court decided these were false allegations. If she had been working with our firm and had consulted us before taking these actions, her case may have ended differently.

We would have suggested that she either drop the allegations or obtain corroborating evidence to back up her claims. For instance, she should have obtained a medical opinion on her child's condition, such as a physician who saw marks on her child that are consistent with child abuse. Without medical evidence, merely seeing marks or bruises on your child - without more - is not enough to provide proof of abuse to the court.

In Summary…

In all of these examples, working with an attorney from the start could have solved these issues or kept them from occurring in the first place. When you come to an attorney after-the-fact, you may have already done damage to your case.

If you see that your marriage is clearly heading for divorce - and working with a therapist or a religious leader cannot save it – it is best to consult with an attorney right away. You can discuss the potential custody and financial issues that could be involved and get legal guidance, even in an initial consultation. Even if you do not plan to file for divorce for another year or more, you should obtain legal counsel now to prepare you for the eventual filing.

CHAPTER 2

UNDERSTANDING DIVORCE SETTLEMENTS IN NEW YORK

Understanding Marital and Divorce Settlement Agreements

A Marital Settlement Agreement - often used interchangeably with terms such as Settlement Agreement or Stipulation of Settlement - is essentially an agreement resolving a divorce matter. This agreement is a binding contract between the involved parties and addresses every issue they may have.

The agreement typically includes a range of "articles" (or sections) that further clarify the scope and detail of the resolution. These may include tax return information, financial disclosure issues, modifications of child support, and other relevant matters. As a result, these agreements tend to be extensive, often ranging from 30 to 70 pages (or more), depending on the complexity of the case and the level of detail required.

Remember, a well-constructed Marital Settlement Agreement is crucial in ensuring a fair and thorough resolution of all divorce-related issues.

What Are the Key Components Typically Included In A Divorce Stipulation Of Settlement?

When creating a settlement agreement for divorce in New York, it's essential to be comprehensive. Below, you can find a list of the main considerations that will need your attention, along with information about the intricacies of each issue.

Property Division

In the context of this conversation, we'll define property as co-ops, condos, plots of land, houses, etc. The main issue you will want to address in your settlement agreement is whether the title is changing - or you are choosing to defer the issue and, if so, for how long.

Unfortunately, I've seen some agreements which only specify that the parties agree to eventually sell the house - but it doesn't set a date. This creates a problem because if the issue is left open-ended, it's very hard to enforce the agreement when one party wants to sell, if there's going to be a buyout, or when the buyout should occur. As such, it's crucial to address all of that in the agreement.

Property Expenses

Next, you'll want to address this question: Who's going to pay all of the expenses in regard to the property pending that sale or buyout? Agreements that don't include provisions to this end can cause major issues.

For example, consider what could happen when it comes time to pay property taxes. If you are living in the house and expect your ex-spouse to chip in for half of the tax obligation only to find out they never had an intention of doing so, you may find yourself in a financial bind.

Personal Property & Financial Assets

In your agreement, it's crucial to address every single bank account - regardless of whether it's a joint or "sole" bank account. Why is this so important? Because people often don't realize their ex-spouse's name is on their account as an authorized user. If your settlement agreement does not specify that each party will agree to remove each other's names as authorized users, you leave a hole open for noncooperation and disagreements later down the road.

Investment Accounts & Retirement Accounts

It is important to address the disposition of all investment accounts and retirement accounts. For example, if there is going to be a qualified domestic relations order ("QDRO")[7] in the retirement account context, you need provisions to address questions like: Who's paying for that? When is it being submitted?

It is advisable to agree on the QDRO drafting service the parties are going to use so they can hit the ground running after the judgment is signed to make sure these important steps are addressed as soon as possible.

Matters Related to the Kids

If children are involved, there are three main areas of consideration: custody, visitation, and child support. It is important to remember here that the more specific you are, the less likely there's going to be a disagreement down the road.

This is particularly true in high-conflict cases, where you will want to have a very lengthy agreement spelling out every aspect of how decisions are made

---

[7] "What is a qualified domestic relations order (qdro)?" HTTPS://WWW.INVESTOPEDIA.COM/TERMS/Q/QDRO.ASP

and provides a game plan of what is going to happen in the event of a disagreement. It is even better if you can include a time frame on when these issues must be resolved.

For example, if you choose to use the professional model on joint custody - where you will defer to the recommendation of a professional on certain decisions which come up in a child's life - you'll want to set a deadline to which the other side must respond (to the email proposing the decision).

To do this, you would include a provision in your settlement agreement saying (for example): "If either parent does not respond to the issue within three days of a triggering email, they waive their right to that decision automatically."

What's more, most parents in high-conflict cases are well advised to use co-parenting apps like Our Family Wizard, Talking Parents, or 2 Houses to facilitate communication. Then, you'll want your agreement to specifically address how these apps will be used, who's going to pay for the app, and more.

In fact, Our Family Wizard even offers suggested language that can be included in the settlement agreement itself to address all the specific details regarding the implementation and use of the Our Family Wizard app in joint custody cases.

Child Support "Add-Ons"

When it comes to child support, you'll need to address all sorts of issues - not only basic child support, but all the add-ons, as well. These "add-ons" can include things like unreimbursed medical care, unreimbursed childcare, unreimbursed education costs, and more.

It's important to spell this out in your agreement so neither party can say, "Well, I don't consider eyeglasses to be a medical expense." Of course, optometric care does typically fall under the rubric of "medical." However, some people - and especially those in high conflict cases - may try to backtrack on any added costs which come up later.

For this reason, you should include specific examples of any additional cost related to child support, including, but not limited to cosmetic surgeries, nose rings, earrings, piercings, and whatever else you might want to address in the future.

Extracurricular Activities

Your divorce settlement agreement should not only dictate who pays for your child's extracurricular activities, but also who transports the child to and from these activities. Additionally, if there's a proposed activity for the child, it's advisable for the parents to agree not to discuss the proposed activity with the children during the decision-making process until the parents have reached an agreement on whether the activity is appropriate.

When incorporating a parent coordinator into a joint custody agreement, it's important to have specific language in your agreement addressing this. In New York, I suggest visiting the court system website - https://www.nycourts.gov/LegacyPDFS/courts/8jd/pdfs/parentcoord/PC_Stip_Order_on_Consent_rev_12-06.pdf.

Maintenance (Alimony)

If you're including alimony in your settlement agreement, you'll need to address all sorts of questions, including: How will the alimony arrangement work? When is it going to end? Under what circumstances, if ever, can it be modified up or down? When, if ever, can it be terminated?

Life Insurance

It's highly recommended for each parent to carry a life insurance policy covering (at least) their portion of anticipated child support. As such, you'll want to address whether each parent will carry a life insurance policy and, if so, for how much.

For example, you could choose to hold a policy covering only the basics, or one accounting for specific child support "add-ons", such as costs associated with private school, college contributions, and more.

Finally, you can add a provision allowing you to "step down" life insurance arrangement. This way, your life insurance obligation can be reduced as your children get older.

As you can see, there are many different considerations when it comes to the key elements of a divorce settlement agreement in New York. At the end of the day, this comes down to the fact that you'll want to craft your divorce settlement agreements to address every conceivable issue that may come up so you don't invite lawyers back into your life later down the road.

Breach of Agreement and Consequences

The agreement will also outline the consequences of breaching the agreement. It may address scenarios like automatic counsel fee awards in case of a breach - but care should be taken with such provisions. Automatic granting of counsel fees can lead to unfair situations, particularly if frivolous violation claims are made.

Deferring Issues for Future Resolution

Consider a situation where the parties do not wish to resolve the issue of child support immediately or there's a separate Family Court case pending. In such cases, the settlement agreement can indicate these issues will be resolved in Family Court.

The deferral of property sale is another common instance. If the parties own a marital residence and are not ready to sell or execute a buyout immediately, they can agree to address this issue at a later stage, such as when the youngest child graduates from high school.

While such deferrals can be incorporated in the settlement agreement, it's important these matters are explicitly stated and not left unresolved.

Why Is a Settlement Agreement Recommended?

While not obligatory, a settlement agreement is considered best practice for divorcing couples. It provides a clear, comprehensive, and legally binding roadmap for the division of assets and custody arrangements. Indeed, some courts or individual Judges/Referees mandate such agreements when children or property is involved. Before proceeding without one, you should verify the specific requirements of your local court.

Even when parties wish to waive division of assets and property, a divorce settlement agreement is still advised to explicitly record such a decision.

Self-Drafted Agreements and Court Forms

In certain situations, couples can utilize various forms available on the court's website, such as maintenance worksheets, child support worksheets, and parenting plans. One should use extreme caution in using divorce agreements obtained off other websites, however. Such agreements may not be state-specific & thus may not be accepted by the court one submits it to. However, if you hire a lawyer, a proper settlement agreement should be drafted.

It's crucial to ensure the attorney you hire is competent and experienced in divorce law. A poorly drafted agreement may fail to address necessary issues and can lead to complications.

Seeking a Second Opinion

If you are in doubt about the quality or sufficiency of your divorce settlement agreement, you should consider seeking a consultation with a reputable divorce attorney. If you're investing in legal representation in the first place, it's essential to ensure you're receiving high-quality service and a thorough, comprehensive agreement.

CHAPTER 3

NEGOTIATING A DIVORCE AGREEMENT IN NEW YORK

How to Negotiate a Divorce Agreement

Negotiating a divorce settlement agreement can be approached in several ways, and typically begins with a comprehensive financial disclosure from each party.

One common practice, particularly when property, assets, or debts are involved, is for both parties to exchange a sworn net worth statement[8]. While not a requirement, this is highly recommended. A net worth statement is a standard financial document in divorce cases disclosing each party's income, assets, and liabilities. This level of transparency helps ensure all marital property and wealth are accounted for, avoiding potential disputes or issues of hidden assets down the line.

An alternative to the net worth statement is to exchange the statements of financial accounts each party has - and then itemize the accounts as a "Schedule" (or rider) to the agreement[9].

Negotiation Methods

Once these statements are exchanged, negotiation can proceed in one of three ways:

---

8 https://www.nycourts.gov/LegacyPDFS/forms/matrimonial/Net-Worth-Statement-Form-Gender-Neutral.pdf

9 That said, the net worth is the recommended path to take. A sample Schedule is found in Appendix B at the back of this book.

1. **Settlement Proposal Letters:** One attorney, after conferring with their client, can produce a settlement proposal letter, outlining the terms their client would accept. This sets a basis for negotiation and allows the attorneys to gauge whether they are in the same ballpark or far apart on key issues.
2. **Direct Attorney Discussions:** Alternatively, instead of initially drafting a written settlement proposal, the attorneys might engage in direct discussion, either via phone calls or emails. This approach can quickly address immediate issues and establish each party's main concerns and demands.
3. **4-Way Settlement Conference:** A more collaborative approach is to conduct a four-way settlement conference involving both parties and their respective attorneys. This could take place in a physical conference room or, increasingly, via digital platforms like Zoom. During this conference, all key issues, such as property division, asset allocation, custody, visitation, child

support, and spousal support, are discussed to try and reach an agreement.

Regardless of the method used, it's crucial to resolve the "basic terms of settlement" before drafting the actual divorce settlement agreement. Drafting a comprehensive settlement agreement before ensuring both parties are willing to settle might result in wasted time and money.

Remember, while most divorces do end in settlement, you don't want to draft a settlement agreement without first confirming both parties are committed to resolving the divorce amicably. The negotiation phase is a crucial step in the divorce process and should be approached with care and thoroughness.

Can a Divorce Agreement Be Modified at Any Time?

The ability to modify a divorce agreement depends on the specific issue. Generally, divorce agreements can be modified regarding custody or visitation issues because the court retains jurisdiction over these matters as long as the children are minors. In New York, this is defined as up to 18 years of age.

The standard for modification always revolves around the best interests of the children. However, the parent seeking to modify must prove a "change of circumstances[10]."

Child support can also be modified. In New York, as of 2010 child support may be automatically modified once every three years, or if there's been a change in income, up or down by 15% - unless the agreement specifically opts out of this provision.

Non-Modifiable Issues: Property and Assets

In theory, provisions relating to property or assets can be modified if the original agreement was unclear. However, this type of modification is considerably more challenging. If the Judge finds the

---

[10] For more information regarding the standards & factors in modifying custody, visitation or support issues, please check out my book "Navigating Your New York Post-Divorce Case: Enforcement & Modification."

agreement clear, they are likely to dismiss any modification request. Therefore, it's crucial to ensure precise terms for property and asset distribution in the original agreement.

For example, in a previous case, a settlement agreement stipulated the husband received 50% of the wife's 401k. However, the wife had a *pension*, not a 401k. The husband's later request for modification to claim 50% of the pension was denied, as the original agreement clearly specified the (nonexistent) 401k – and waived all other assets not otherwise addressed.

This case underscores the importance of clarity and full disclosure when establishing a divorce settlement agreement. Insisting on financial statement exchange can offer a safety net to argue for modification if the other party has misled you about their assets. However, it's best to confirm all details to avoid misunderstandings or misrepresentations. One way to do that is to request statements from each of the financial accounts which a party discloses on the net worth statement. This way, if a party claims on the net worth to have a 401k - but the statement reveals it's actually a pension - then the agreement can incorporate the more precise language.

What Happens If One Party Refuses To Sign The Stipulation Of Settlement Agreement In New York? Are There Any Legal Remedies Or Consequences?

The straightforward answer is no, both parties must reach an agreement for a settlement to be valid. If one party declines to sign off on a settlement, the case remains unresolved.

In such situations, it's essential to identify the specific points of disagreement and work towards finding a compromise that both parties can accept, possibly with the assistance of a mediator or through court proceedings. Occasionally, if the parties agree on most terms but have a few outstanding disagreements, I approach the judge for an "advisory opinion."

At this stage, if both parties and both attorneys agree to seek the judge's advisory opinion, the judge is free to intervene and provide recommendations based on the information provided. The judge may say something like, "I can't prejudge the trial, but based on the information, here's how I recommend resolving the deadlock."

Sometimes, judges may delegate this task to a court attorney, which is perfectly acceptable. The key point is that if one party does not follow through with the agreement, both sides must either reach an agreement on different terms or inform the judge that the case will proceed to trial.

How Does A New York Court Typically Review And Approve A Stipulation Of Settlement Agreement In A Divorce Case? What Factors Do They Consider?

When it comes to divorce settlement agreements, the court's primary concern is ensuring that all the crucial elements are addressed. As such, the court tends to approve most properly executed agreements.

For example, I've encountered situations where agreements were sent back because the opposing counsel forgot to specify who would cover the child's medical insurance. The court typically requires such details to be clearly outlined in either an addendum to the agreement or an affidavit to ensure that nothing essential is omitted.

This is just one example, but when the court finds that certain important elements are missing from a standard settlement agreement, they will send it back. It's crucial to understand that, according to the law, the court cannot make changes to an agreement. So, the court's role is not to examine the agreement and determine, for instance, whether the visitation arrangement is in the best interest of the children, as that would be beyond its authority in such matters.

The court carefully examines agreements to ensure they align with public policy and the law. For example, it's essential to clearly mention in your agreement that child support can be changed once alimony ends. If you forget to include this, the court might step in and say, "Your agreement needs this provision to follow the law." In my experience, I rarely encounter such issues, but there are cases where people consult me because they missed adding a proper acknowledgment in their agreements.

In many cases, the court process is relatively straightforward once the agreement is well-prepared. So you should ensure that your attorneys have the necessary expertise and a track record of successfully securing agreement approvals. It's essential that they're not newcomers to divorce law, as sometimes personal injury attorneys may not possess the required knowledge for divorce settlements. Being cautious in your choice is crucial.

What Are The Potential Advantages Of Reaching A Stipulation Of Settlement Agreement In New York Divorce Case As Opposed To Going To Trial?

The number one advantage of settlements is that they're a sure thing. By going to trial and putting all or some of your issues in the hands of the judge, you're risking the judge coming up with a resolution that's not ideal for either of the parties.

Another advantage of settlement agreements is the cost; it's far less expensive to reach a settlement than it is to proceed to trial. In many senses, trials are just formalities. Why? Because by the time a case gets to trial, the judge has seen the parties, heard their arguments over pre-trial hearings and conferences, and has a pretty good idea as to how they're going to decide the case anyway.

If you proceed to trial in the Greater New York City area with a good divorce attorney, you're conservatively looking at about $30- $50,000 in trial costs. In fact, you could be looking at an even higher bill than that if the trial deals with high-net-worth individuals, involves complex issues, or needs a decision on both financial issues as well as custody and visitation matters.

Another aspect to consider is the potential costs associated with a trial. These expenses may include fees for an attorney representing the child or children, payments to experts, witness fees, and the issuance of subpoenas. All of these factors can significantly increase the overall cost of the trial, expenses that can be avoided if you opt for a settlement instead.

In conclusion, the main reasons to strongly consider pursuing a divorce settlement rather than going to trial are twofold: first, the potential cost savings, as avoiding trial-related expenses can be significant; and second, the fact that the overwhelming majority of divorces, approximately 95 to 98%, ultimately reach resolution through a settlement agreement at some stage.

What Are the Common Mistakes That Someone Should Be Aware Of When Negotiating Or Signing The Settlement Agreement In Their New York Divorce Case Without An Experienced Family Law Attorney?

First and foremost, it's in your best interest to avoid negotiating or signing a divorce agreement without the help of an experienced divorce lawyer. A lot of people think they can get a typical divorce settlement online, but it's important to be very wary of these websites.

If you have the resources to hire a good divorce attorney, it's a wise move. A skilled attorney can help you create a solid agreement upfront, preventing the need for lawyers to revisit your case due to unresolved issues in the future. It's an investment that can save you from ongoing legal disputes.

Another concern is when someone with sufficient financial resources opts for a budget divorce attorney. I'm currently handling a case where the wife earns between $200,000 to $300,000 annually, and, without any disrespect to the opposing counsel, it's obvious that she chose a cheap divorce attorney.

Now, when I say "obviously" it's because the attorney in question drafted a parenting agreement to resolve custody and visitation issues that was clearly subpar. It appeared they had used a form from the court's website which is typically intended for indigent individuals.

In this situation, it's clear the person could have easily afforded a good divorce attorney to draft a high-quality agreement, but instead, they ended up with a subpar one. Of course, it's possible the party might not even be fully aware of how inadequate the agreement is and how poorly their attorney performed.

However, this underscores the importance of researching an attorney beforehand by asking critical questions like: What percentage of your cases involve divorce? How long have you been practicing divorce law? Simply claiming to be a divorce attorney isn't sufficient, and due diligence in selecting the right legal representation is essential.

For this reason, you should consider inquiring about an attorney's background and experience, including any recent career changes or transitions. It’s totally fine to ask questions about the percentage of divorce cases they handle compared to other practice areas, the duration of their experience in divorce law, and their current caseload is a wise approach.

Finally, keep this in mind: If an attorney's caseload is excessively high (100 cases+), it can impact their ability to give proper attention to drafting agreements or closely supervise paralegals who might assist in your case.

How Does the Enforcement Of A Stipulation Of Settlement Agreement Work In New York If One Party Fails To Adhere To Terms Or Obligations?

Unless there's an urgent situation, the party claiming a violation should send a default notice letter. This letter can be straightforward and sent via email or through the communication method specified in the agreement, such as Our Family Wizard. In the letter, you should bring attention to the alleged violation, request a resolution of the issue, and inform them that if they don't comply, your next step may involve possibly filing a violation case.

Why is it important to say that your next move could possibly involve going to court? Consider this hypothetical: On one occasion, your child's father is late for pick up. Your agreement says he's supposed to pick up the child at 10 a.m. on Saturdays, but he's not there & eventually shows up at 11 a.m.

While this is a technical violation of the agreement, the party alleging the violation would be a fool to run into court and ask for the father to be held in contempt of court. In this situation, the Judge would probably just tell the father to show up on time from now on and dismiss the case. The result? You just wasted time going to court for nothing.

With scenarios like these, you really want a pattern of lateness and "minor violations." If you're not sure whether something is minor or major, in terms of a violation of the agreement, the best move is to consult with a good divorce attorney who can help you get clarity.

What Role Do Attorneys Play in The Negotiation And Drafting Of A Stipulation Of Settlement Agreement In New York Divorce Cases?

Divorce attorneys play a pivotal role in negotiating and drafting settlement agreements in New York. To start, the attorney will first exchange net worth statements for each party. Then, it will be on the attorneys to kick off the negotiation process.

In most cases, this will take place via an exchange of letters, emails, or even phone. This step allows both sides to find out whether there is any basic agreement on the terms of the settlement. In other cases, the parties may set up a four-way conference, including the two parties and their two attorneys. In these conferences, the attorneys take a relatively active role.

An additional role of an attorney comes into play in the form of providing guidance. Should negotiations fall apart, the case will go in front of a judge. As such, your attorney will be a key resource from whom you can get insight into the law and what you would be likely to see happen in court should the negotiation process stall.

CHAPTER 4

THE ROLE OF PARENT COORDINATORS & FACILITATORS

What Are Parent Coordinators and Parent Facilitators In New York State?

Divorce is always a difficult time, doubly so for parents. That is why some will call on the services of a parent coordinator to help handle some of the touchier topics.

A parent coordinator or facilitator, however, is not the same as a mediator. Unlike a divorce mediator, a parent coordinator is only allowed to discuss matters of child custody and visitation. On the other hand, unlike a mediator, the coordinator's role can be more proactive and they can make strong recommendations, rather than merely listening and helping the parents arrive at a compromise by themselves.

That said, the role of a parent coordinator is limited. Unlike a mediator, they cannot help with any financial issues whatsoever. So if child support, alimony, or asset distribution comes up during the discussion, they will not be permitted to address those issues. The other main limitation is that the parent coordinator or facilitator's role is dependent on the initial divorce settlement agreement between the parents (or court order of referral).

How Is the Role Of A Parent Coordinator Or Facilitator Defined During A Divorce?

Unlike a mediator, whose role is always to help parties come to an agreement, a parent coordinator's role is defined during the divorce settlement agreement.

A parent coordinator or facilitator can be empowered by the divorce settlement to make decisions (more akin to an arbitrator) on behalf of the parties. The exact degree of this will depend on the drafting and wording of the divorce settlement (or court order of referral), but this means that the coordinator can be given any degree of power from recommendations only to binding decisions both parents have agreed to follow.

While they can never be given the power to discuss or decide on financial matters, or really any subject beyond custody and visitation matters, their ability to decide matters (or at least provide strong recommendations) for both parties can be made stronger than that of a mediator.

How Does a Parent Coordinator Or Facilitator Make Decisions About Child Custody Or Visitations?

In a situation in which the parent coordinator has been empowered to make decisions after a divorce there are a number of steps they will take to ensure it is the best possible decision:

- The parent coordinator will often start by meeting all the parties involved.
- They may also get in touch independently with any healthcare, childcare, or mental health professionals if they are relevant to the particular decision.
- They usually review any documents that are relevant to the particular decision.

Once they have covered all the information and background required, they will be able to make an informed decision, always with the best interest of the child in mind. If it is a joint custody dispute, they will usually make a recommendation to the parties (often in writing) so that the parents can be guided by that decision.

If the agreement between the parents (or court order of referral) has empowered the coordinator, then their decisions are to be implemented. No agreement however can make the coordinator's recommendation absolutely binding, so if one party adamantly disagrees with it they can still try to persuade a Judge to rule otherwise. Along these lines, the divorce settle or referral order will usually state the parent coordinator's decision/recommendation will be "presumptively implemented," thus giving the disagreeing parent an avenue with the Judge if s/he adamantly disagrees.

However, if the agreement presumptively defers the decision to the coordinator, whichever parent disagrees with their recommendation is going to have a tough time arguing to the Judge that it should not be followed. Nevertheless, if you ever do find yourself in such a bind, having an experienced and qualified lawyer on your side can make all the difference.

Most of the time, however, a parent coordinator or facilitator will be able to have a significant positive impact on post-divorce disputes over child custody or visitation and can be a useful tool for moving forward with the child's best interest in mind.

How Does the Parent Coordinator Help Resolve Disputes And Improve Communication Between Parents Involved In A Family Law Matter?

One of the very first things any parent coordinator is going to do is discuss everything with both parties. Nowadays this is often done via Zoom, but sometimes it can be more helpful to conduct in person, as it is the first step towards a proactive and positive resolution.

Since the goal of the parent coordinator is to resolve the dispute, the first step is to review it, and, especially if it is a post-judgment issue, to get as broad a view as possible of the full context. Whether the parent coordinator is new to the case or familiar with it, they will often start with several key questions to get all of the relevant background information:

- Were there domestic violence issues raised and or sustained at the trial level?

- Were there drug and alcohol issues raised or sustained by the judge?
- Did one party or the other have a mental illness?
- Was there a forensic psychological evaluation done?

Sometimes the parent coordinator may need to go beyond just asking, however, and do some digging of their own. For example, they might need to make an application to the Judge so that they can receive the forensic report that was done during the divorce so that they can be better informed in terms of making decisions, especially if they are empowered to (presumptively) make decisions for the parties.

Being fully informed, after all, is the foundation of good decision-making, and the parent coordinator will always want to make the best possible recommendation for you, and most importantly, your child(ren).

How Long Will a Parent Coordinator Or Facilitator Take To Make Their Decision?

Given the breadth of information required to come to a decision, a parent coordinator may require more than one session. This is especially true if either party held back in terms of providing all relevant information beforehand.

However, unlike a full-blown mediation which will also need to cover financial issues, a parent coordinator's more limited scope allows the process to go faster. Because they are deciding or recommending on a very limited issue or set of issues, a parent coordinator will generally only need two or three sessions.

What Are the Qualifications or Credentials Required For Someone To Become A Parent Coordinator In Family Law?

The exact qualifications or credentials required to become a parent coordinator or facilitator does vary somewhat based on the county or judicial district. Generally, however, they are required to receive a specific certification, and once they do, they will generally be on a court-certified list.

Just as each county or judicial district will have a court-certified list of mediators, if they differentiate between mediators and parent coordinators, they will have a separate list for them. In the counties where they do not, if someone is certified to be a mediator, they're also presumptively certified to be a parent coordinator.

The court list[11], however, is just the list of coordinators or mediators which the court may assign. Any mediator or attorney who has undergone the appropriate certification from a mediation training organization could be hired independently as your coordinator. Usually, this certification process is done through a 48 or 60-hour course that covers the legal, practical, and psychological background for the mediator role.

This certification is important, however, as you do not want someone unqualified to handle such delicate yet important matters without the necessary training. That is why you should always ask where a prospective mediator or coordinator you are considering received their certification from - or better still, ask to see it directly. If they cannot produce it or

---

[11] https://ww2.nycourts.gov/ip/adr/MedDirectory.shtml

give you the name, that is a bad sign, and you should probably move on to a new family law attorney.

After all, given the role and responsibilities of a parent coordinator or facilitator, you want the most qualified, unbiased, reliable, and experienced family law attorney to handle your case.

What Issues or Conflicts Do Parent Coordinators Address in Family Law Cases?

Parent coordinators, sometimes also called facilitators, are trained attorneys and mediators who help make recommendations for solutions to some of the delicate or thorny problems which emerge after a divorce.

Most of the time, a parent coordinator is going to be called in for joint custody issues. These are the decisions that come up regularly in the life of the child, but which their parents disagree over. For instance, medical decisions, educational decisions, and extracurricular activity decisions could all be the source of conflicts and are common issues parent coordinators will deal with.

More rarely, a parent coordinator may even have to deal with access issues.

Let us consider a couple of examples. In one post-divorce settlement agreement, the wording is unclear on an aspect of joint custody such as failing to specify particular pickup and drop-off locations for regular visits. And the parents end up with issues, questions, or conflict about what happens if the child is off from school and the agreement does not address that. Another family might be arguing over what happens during summer vacation when their agreement does not address that.

These are the kind of issues where a parent coordinator can step in and guide the parties through the process of solving them. Depending on the wording of the divorce settlement agreement, the parent coordinator may also be empowered to make the decision themselves.

While some might consider that presumptive, it can certainly allow for a faster and less conflictual resolution. In addition, even if so empowered, such a determination is not permanent. Either parent can usually appeal to the Judge if they adamantly disagree with a recommendation to the parent coordinator - though doing so does require going to court.

What Are the Benefits Of Involving A Parent Coordinator In A Family Law Case?

There are several benefits to choosing parent-coordinator mediation to help resolve a visitation dispute or joint custody disagreement. Especially when compared to taking it to court.

One of the biggest benefits is that parent coordination often happens on your time. Courts will only handle a dispute between the hours of 9-5, which means you are likely to have to take off either a morning, an afternoon, or both, from work to go. The parent coordinating process on the other hand, can take place during evenings or on weekends.

Furthermore, in the greater New York City area, most courts and Judges are going back to in-person appearances (i.e., post-pandemic). Mediators and parent coordinators, on the other hand, often accommodate Zoom sessions. You may not even have to go into an office at all.

It is also important to remember that by working with both parties, parent coordinators can help avoid more conflictual solutions. In addition to speaking to both parties, a parent coordinator will also often speak to the relevant professional involved (such as a doctor or educator) and get reports to guide their decision-making process to come to the best possible decision. They are impartial and unbiased, their only goal is the smooth resolution of the conflict for the best interest of the child(ren) involved.

The final benefit, however, is cost. If you have to go to court, this means each party is hiring an attorney and going into court for a fight that could take several sessions. Invariably, the costs are at least double those of jointly retaining a parent coordinator or mediator. Therefore, when parent coordination is successful, everyone will save time and money.

What Happens If Parent Coordination Fails?

While parent coordination can help resolve most issues that arise, there are exceptions. Even when the post-divorce agreement requires both parties to follow the mediator's decision, they can be contested.

This does, however, mean that, unlike a court-based solution, parent coordination is not final and irreversible. Yes, contesting it might require going to court (with the costs that ensue), but doing so would give you another chance at a more favorable outcome if the first was truly unacceptable.

Overall, for most post-divorce parents, and especially those facing minor issues, parent coordination remains a particularly effective and practical solution. For post-judgment issues in particular, when the conflictual part of the divorce, no one wants to open the can of worms all over again for much smaller issues. That is where the parent coordinator comes into play. And certainly, when a minor dispute arises months or even years after a divorce, it is worth giving a parent coordinator a shot before moving for any more drastic or costly solutions.

CHAPTER 5

NEW YORK FAMILY LAW MEDIATION: THE BASICS EVERY FAMILY NEEDS TO KNOW

In family law, perhaps more so than in almost any other area of law, conflicts are inevitable. In family law, conflicts are inherently personal already. Mediation is a legal tool to help two parties reach an agreement or compromise without going through court. This process can be extremely advantageous, but does have its limits and disadvantages. This chapter is designed to answer basic questions about how mediation is used in New York family law, including:

- What Mediation is, how it works, and when it can be used.
- The costs and restrictions of mediation as it is used in family law in New York.
- Some examples of how mediation can work, or not work, in a divorce settlement case.

What Is Mediation and Who Is the Mediator?

Mediation is a process where two (or very rarely, three or more) parties will meet with a neutral person to help them come to an agreement. Most of the time that's an attorney, though it technically does not have to be one. The parties are free to use anyone who is certified to be a mediator.

It is generally recommended, however, that the mediator be an attorney with at least some experience in the specific legal issues at stake and in the dispute they are helping to resolve.

What Makes for A Good Mediator in Family Law In New York?

In New York, only certified mediators are allowed to conduct mediation. This is vital as the mediator must be capable of staying neutral while remaining accountable for doing so.

Mediation certification training is usually a 48 to 60-hour course that family law practitioners will take. In a nutshell, it focuses on how to work out or attempt to work out an agreement, as well as how to draft it. The mediator does not generally draft any forms other than the agreement itself.

As such, one of the things you will want to check when choosing a mediator is where they got their certification from. Often this will be prominently on display as a diploma or plaque, but if they are unable to answer, it might be best to choose a different mediator!

Do I Need a Court-Certified Mediator for My Family Law Dispute Mediation?

New York family law courts have a separate list of court-certified mediators[12]. You are not obliged to choose one of these for your dispute.

The only difference between the court-certified list and other certified mediators is that a Judge or Referee in your divorce case or Family Court case must make the referral to the court-certified mediator directly. When seeking your own "privately-retained" mediator, there is no obligation to choose from this list.

If a mediator is on the court-certified list, they have to agree to a whole set of rules, including about their hourly rate. In Westchester, for example, they are limited to $400 an hour (as of 2023) - which is often a substantial decrease from the $500 to $800+ an experienced divorce attorney can otherwise bill.

---

[12] https://ww2.nycourts.gov/ip/adr/MedDirectory.shtml

What Is the Role of a Mediator in Family Law In New York State?

Mediation is all about reaching an agreement without having to go through the time and expense of court. By negotiating through the neutral third party, the mediator, individuals are able to come to a compromise they can both agree on and proceed with the family law matter at stake. The mediator does not necessarily replace the need for a lawyer of your own, nor will they handle the majority of the procedural aspects of the divorce case itself.

For example, let us say you hire a mediator to do a divorce settlement. The mediator will not actually file the divorce case in court. Nor will they draft the "judgment package," which includes the judgment of divorce terminating the marriage. Instead, the mediator will draft the "settlement agreement" (a/k/a "stipulation of settlement") - or a separation agreement if you are not ready to proceed with the divorce.

In addition, they will walk you through all of the issues at stake in the case, such as...

- Child custody,
- Child support,
- Child visitation,
- Asset distribution,
- Property distribution,
- Debt distribution, and
- Maintenance (a/k/a alimony).

After going over the issues at stake in your case, they will present you with a menu of options. Once they have found options both parties can agree on - which can sometimes take several rounds of negotiation (and more rarely, several mediation sessions) - they will produce the agreement you have settled on.

What Is the Difference Between A Mediator and An Attorney? Do I Need Both?

The key difference between a mediator and an attorney is the mediator is not there to give you legal advice. Unlike an attorney, a mediator is never supposed to answer questions such as "Should I do this" or "Is this option in my best interest"? The mediator is supposed to remain neutral throughout the entire process.

Instead, they essentially guide you through the process of reaching your own agreement. They will not tell you what you might get if you take an issue to a Judge, as such questions are best handled by your own family law attorney. If you reach the point where you have those questions in the process of mediation and do not already have one, you need to go out and get your own attorney. It is vital to have both the legal advice an attorney can provide and the guidance toward compromise a mediator can offer for mediation to work well.

What Does a Family Law Mediation Process Look Like In New York?

Usually, the process of mediation is conducted over the course of several sessions, with the aim of reaching an agreement on all the issues. This is often referred to as the "basic term sheet."

At the end of mediation, the mediator will distribute the term sheet to each spouse (or each party if it's a family court case) and will ask a series of key questions once you have discussed everything in mediation, such as…

- Are these terms what you are agreeing to?
- Do you want or need anything else?
- Do you have any other questions?
- Do you need any other legal advice[13]?

Once they are satisfied everyone understands and accepts the terms, the mediator will draft the actual settlement agreement - or the parenting agreement if it is a Family Court case (such as custody or visitation disputes). Either way, they will then distribute it to both parties.

Everyone is then encouraged to bring that agreement over to their attorneys. Their attorneys will look it over, discuss it with each party, give them legal advice on the agreement, and possibly suggest changes. If they want any changes, they come back to the mediator and launch another round of discussion. Once both

---

[13] Again, the mediator cannot give legal advice, but should nevertheless ask that question of the parties before they execute the agreement. If either party answers in the affirmative, the mediator should stop the process & ask the party to consult an attorney before proceeding further.

parties reach the point where they are fine with what's been drafted by the mediator, it's just a matter of signing it before a notary public, and the mediation is done.

What Are the Advantages and Disadvantages of Mediation for Resolving Family Law Disputes?

When mediation works, both parties end up saving considerable amounts of money compared to the "regular" process of going through a divorce case. After all, you can split the mediation fee and will need far fewer billable attorney hours. And mediation works, on average, roughly 50% of the time.

Unfortunately, when it does not work, you will end up spending *even more* money than if you had just gone through the regular divorce process from the very beginning. This is because the mediator will get paid irrespective of whether an agreement is reached. As such, when mediation fails, the parties essentially go back to their respective attorneys and begin the settlement negotiation all over again. In effect, the money you spent on the mediator will have been "wasted."

So, before taking that gamble, ask yourself how reasonable you think your spouse is going to be in reaching an agreement.

Mediators will often help by doing an initial screening to avoid cases where there has been relatively recent domestic violence or where there are coercive control issues. At that point, each party really ought to have their own attorney, and mediation is not the correct approach.

Otherwise, if two reasonable, rational people come into the case – and who are cooperative but just cannot live under the same roof and need to terminate the marriage - mediation can certainly work wonders and save everyone considerable time and cost.

Can Mediation Be Used to Create Marital Agreements As Well?

If one defines "marital agreement" as a prenuptial agreement, postnuptial agreement, separation agreement, or stipulation of settlement (a/k/a divorce settlement agreement), then mediation can absolutely be used.

A mediator can do the same exact job a divorce attorney or family law attorney can do, with the end result of reaching any of those agreements *including* prenuptial agreements. There is, however, one major difference. Unlike an attorney – and as stated above - a mediator is not there to give legal advice. In fact, they cannot, as they must remain neutral throughout the process. If at any point in the process of reaching one of those agreements, either party or both have legal advice questions, they have to stop the mediation process and direct the question to his/her attorney.

With that caveat aside, a mediator can draft the agreement and have the parties execute it. If the mediator is a notary public, they can even notarize the parties' signatures.

What Are the Key Benefits of Using Mediation to Negotiate and Draft A Marital Agreement?

The most immediate benefit enjoyed by anyone using mediation is saving money. The retainer for a (good) mediator in the greater New York City area might cost anywhere between $5,000 and $10,000. You are still going to save money compared to trying to do the same process with each party spending $5,000 to $10,000 for their own separate attorneys (& for high net worth and/or complex cases, initial fees can be even more than that). When it works, mediation is clearly a cost-saving measure.

Mediation is also a non-adversarial setting, which inherently favors the spirit of compromise. Mediation often consists of two parties either getting together on a Zoom call or in the mediator's conference room, and it tends to be very low-key and amicable.

If the mediator perceives there is tension, such as fear, mistrust, or anger, most mediators are going to stop that process, as it is unlikely to work. The mediator will ask everyone to be amicable, rational, and reasonable to move forward. If not, then they will refund the balance of the retainer and leave you in the hands of separate attorneys, or your fates in the hands of Judges and litigation.

Is Mediation a Sufficiently Trustworthy and Thorough Process For Drafting Marital Agreements?

While Mediation is less adversarial than litigation, it does entail the exchange of crucial information, including the verification of the parties' respective finances. It is quite appropriate for parties to exchange net worth statements, for example, when drafting marital agreements.

In the mediation process, either side can ask for the verification of amounts in bank accounts, investment accounts, or retirement accounts. Indeed, doing so is recommended, as you should not reach an agreement without understanding the situation and stakes. Likewise, it is not recommended to reach a settlement if you have no idea what the other person has in their bank account or going off a simple oral statement from them.

It is vital to have such information verified to avoid sticky legal situations further down the line. For example, consider the situation where a party says they have only $10,000 in an account - only to find out they actually had $30,000 after the agreement was signed because they lied in the mediation process. These situations can get very difficult, especially if you have already signed an agreement. This is why, even during mediation, full verification measures are encouraged.

What Are Some Common Issues or Topics That Couples Can Address During Mediation In New York State?

The issues that are addressed in mediation are the same exact issues addressed in the regular divorce or Family Court process. In fact, having an agreement negotiated ahead of time through mediation can even avoid most of the issues that come up later during a divorce.

It is pretty much a given if you are going through a divorce that both will agree on the termination of marriage. What you are really attempting to resolve are all the other issues that can exist between the two parties. These can include…

- Custody, visitation, and/or child support for any children.

- Spousal maintenance, i.e., alimony.
- Asset, property, and debt distribution.
- The valuation of other assets (businesses, professional practices, etc.).
- Dealing with a shared or individually owned business.

All such issues can still be resolved in the process of mediation - and many, or even all, could be agreed on even before the marriage through prenuptial agreements.

The mediator can even find experts, such as forensic accountants, to value a business or value a particular asset (e.g., a pension or other retirement account) which comes up during the mediation process.

Assuming both parties reach an agreement on all these issues, the mediation process will go considerably smoother than traditional litigation, and at a substantially lower cost. Doing so before marriage could mean starting the relationship off right - on even grounds of transparency, compromise, and trust. And if the marriage ends up failing, well, you will have saved costs on divorce procedures as well!

What Role Does a Mediator Play in Family Law Negotiations?

Family law struggles can be delicate. The issues at stake are important, the circumstances inevitably life-changing, and the emotions of many parties running high. To do a good job of bringing parties together toward a compromise, a mediator has to be clear, honest, and purposeful.

Their work always begins by setting up the process and explaining what mediation is. A good mediator will use this time to set the tone, build trust and rapport, and begin assessing the problems in play.

The next step is often a questionnaire form[14]. Each party must fill them out, with the understanding they will be shared with the other party. Everyone needs to know

---

[14] See the Appendix at the back of this book for a sample questionnaire.

everything, transparency and honesty are essential to good mediation. Secrets are for attorney-client privileges – not amicable mediation. Mediators must remain neutral and make sure both parties are on the same page and receive all communications within the mediation process.

This ensures a fairness individuals might not find in a traditional trial when dealing solely with attorneys.

How Does a Mediator Facilitate Communication And Ensure A Fair And Balanced Negotiation Process?

Another tool any good mediator will use is meticulous note-taking. They will take careful notes of every single mediation session and may send each party a copy so they can keep track of the progress of mediation.

You do not want to pick up after two or three weeks and have people unsure of where they left off. Those notes ensure everyone knows exactly where they left off and what was discussed or decided so far in the mediation process. This not only facilitates further communication but also helps ensure a fair and balanced negotiation.

Transparency is also important between parties. For example, if there is any money involved (such as during a divorce or even pre-nuptial agreement), parties will be asked to exchange net worth statements and statements from all of their sole accounts. If one spouse has an account solely in their name, they will be asked to share a statement of its worth, to verify any oral declarations. Such transparency is essential and it is the job of the mediator to encourage and facilitate it to ensure a fair and balanced process.

Unlike in a courtroom, however, a mediator cannot enforce such transparency.

What Happens When Parties Do Not Wish to Share Information During Mediation?

A mediator will generally ask for full transparency, especially on any issue or topic related to the dispute or settlement. Unlike in litigation, however, the parties can essentially do whatever they want to do.

If both parties say they do not need to exchange bank statements, it's not a problem. The mediator will tell everyone what is recommended, but if the parties don't want to go through the time and expense of doing so, that is their decision. The mediator will simply put into writing in the eventual agreement that both parties were recommended to exchange the given statements or documents and they declined that recommendation. This absolves the mediator of responsibility for any dishonesty by the parties but can sometimes.

What Happens If an Agreement Cannot Be Reached Through Mediation?

If parties cannot come to an agreement through compromise and mediation, they are left with the original alternative: going to court & pursing litigation. If they have already filed a divorce or Family Court process, then they will simply continue with the case before the Judge or Referee.

If there's no pending case when mediation fails, the parties are simply recommended to file their divorce or petitions in Family Court and proceed with litigation.

If the mediation failed early enough in the process, they will also be reimbursed the remainder of the retainer they paid, so those costs are not lost if the mediation goes nowhere.

Are The Agreements Reached During Mediation Legally Binding? What Is the Process To Make Them Enforceable?

Once an agreement reached through mediation is signed, acknowledged, and notarized, it is a binding legal contract between the parties. However, there are some differences in what a mediated agreement can legally do.

For example, one key difference between a mediation agreement and a court order is that a mediation agreement cannot garnish wages. If there is a child support issue or unpaid alimony the other party cannot take the agreement to a sheriff and ask them to garnish this person's wages because they defaulted on the agreement. Instead, to deal with such an issue or other similar constraints, they have to turn the agreement into a court order.

To do so, they would have to go to Family Court and get an order of child support or spousal support, with the mediated agreement incorporated into it[15]. When the petition is filed, the agreement can be attached as "Exhibit A," showing that the other party already signed a mediation agreement several months ago. Since the spouse is failing to pay, the court can then be asked to issue an order based on the agreement.

Likewise, with a married couple, they would simply file a divorce case and submit the agreement to the Judge as part of the "judgment package." Then they can ask the Judge to issue a judgment of divorce incorporating the agreement - which can be enforced like any other court order.

How Does Mediation Differ from Traditional Attorney-Led Negotiations?

The key difference is you have a neutral attorney working with you as opposed to two

---

[15] The form for same is here: https://www.nycourts.gov/LegacyPDFS/FORMS/familycourt/pdfs/4-1.pdf

adversarial attorneys in the traditional divorce route. While this can facilitate coming to an agreement, there are some limitations.

A mediator cannot give legal advice to the parties without breaching the condition of neutrality. The party wanting legal advice will have to consult with their own attorney before returning to the negotiation table.

Moreover, at times a recalcitrant party may withhold financial disclosure - and without the imminent threat of contested litigation - may be in a better position to do so in the mediation context.

Mediation is a process that could very well save you considerable time and money if you feel the other party is going to be reasonable and rational. It is often worth a shot to try mediation - if it works, you will end up saving money and more often than not have a considerably more pleasant and amicable experience.

CHAPTER 6

PRENUPTIAL & POSTNUPTIAL AGREEMENTS IN NEW YORK

What Is A Prenuptial Agreement And What Are Its Main Purposes?

A prenuptial agreement refers to a contract entered into by two individuals planning to get married. It serves primarily two functions:

1. Capture current assets: It documents the financial assets and property both parties hold before marriage. As you might be aware, couples generally

enter a marriage full of love and optimism, hardly considering the possibility of divorce. Yet it's an unfortunate fact that approximately 50% of marriages do end in divorce. Financial institutions maintain records for about seven years, leading to difficulties in divorce cases where proof of premarital assets is required after a more extended period. For example, individuals might struggle to demonstrate the premarital component of their investments and retirement accounts if they have not kept up-to-date records. This is where a prenuptial agreement becomes invaluable.

2. Determine asset distribution upon divorce: A prenuptial agreement helps establish how assets and property will be distributed in the event of divorce. While generally divorce law provides for an equal 50-50 division of assets, your prenuptial agreement can propose a different arrangement. For instance, let's consider a scenario where a future husband owns a house before marriage. In a typical divorce situation, the wife would be entitled to a share of the equity build-up (e.g., pay down of the mortgage

during the marriage) and active appreciation of the property. However, with a prenuptial agreement, you can decide to deviate from this standard rule.

What Issues Can Be Addressed In The Prenuptial Agreement?

Prenuptial agreements commonly address financial concerns, such as the division of assets and property, and spousal maintenance. However, their scope is broad and can cover virtually any issue. You can include provisions concerning:

- Custody and visitation rights of existing children
- Child support for existing children
- Distribution of current debts and those incurred during the marriage
- Handling of assets that gain value or are acquired during the marriage
- Addressing how assets which exist as of time of marriage are to be divided (if at all)

Essentially, a prenuptial agreement can encompass any clause that might be included in a separation agreement or divorce settlement agreement.

Are Prenuptial Agreements Enforceable In Court?

Prenuptial agreements are indeed enforceable in court - assuming they're done correctly - and thus functioning as binding contracts between the parties involved. In theory, one party could take legal action against the other for a breach of contract. However, this approach is seldom used.

Usually, if a prenuptial agreement needs enforcing, it indicates some form of marital discord. In such cases, attorneys typically recommend the client initiate a divorce or legal separation case. Both proceedings can incorporate the prenuptial agreement, thereby facilitating its enforcement within the context of the divorce or legal separation.

Once the prenuptial agreement becomes a court order, it can then be enforced via a post-judgment application. During the proceedings, if the parties don't wish to dismiss any clauses of the prenuptial agreement, negotiations can take place to resolve any outstanding payments, asset distributions, property divisions, or alimony due as per the agreement.

These negotiations can result in a subsequent agreement that would be incorporated into the judgment of separation or judgment of divorce, further reinforcing the enforceability of the initial prenuptial agreement.

How Long Does It Generally Take to Draft A Prenuptial Agreement?

The time required to draft a prenuptial agreement can vary significantly based on the complexities of the specific case. Upon receiving the initial information and understanding your desires for the prenuptial agreement, one should generally exchange formal net worth statements with your partner. This process can be time-consuming, but it is recommended for a clear financial understanding. However, if you are comfortable with your partner's disclosure, this step can be bypassed, and you can instead include bullet-point lists of assets, property, and debts in the agreement (usually attached to the agreement as a "schedule").

Once these preliminary steps are completed, the core of the prenuptial agreement can be drafted. Typically, this process, including adjustments and refinements, takes about two to four weeks. However, the timeline can extend if formal net worth statements are prepared - and thus will depend on how quickly these can be completed. Some couples may take as little as a week, while others may need well over a month.

If your wedding ceremony is imminent and you are under time pressure, it's important to expedite the process to ensure the prenuptial agreement is finalized well before the wedding. Presenting a prenuptial agreement to your soon-to-be spouse just before the wedding is not recommended, as it may be perceived as coercion and increase the chance of the agreement being invalidated by a Judge in the future.

Ideally, your prenuptial agreement should be completed at least a week before the wedding ceremony. Therefore, if you're hiring an attorney, it's best to start the process at least a couple of months prior to the wedding date. This way, you can ensure there's sufficient time to draft and finalize the agreement without any last-minute rush.

Can A Prenuptial Agreement Be Modified or Revoked After Marriage?

Yes, a prenuptial agreement can be modified or revoked after marriage, typically upon the mutual consent of both parties. Most prenuptial agreements emphasize their binding nature and specify that any modifications must be formalized through a similar agreement. This new agreement should be professionally drafted, signed, notarized, and acknowledged by both parties.

However, if only one party desires to modify the agreement and the other opposes, modifications become challenging without judicial intervention. If you wish to change the terms of your prenuptial agreement after the marriage and your partner does not consent, then depending on the importance of the changes, it might necessitate legal separation or divorce proceedings.

In such cases, it's important to consult an attorney to explore your options[16]. Remember, any agreement requires both parties to be in sync, and if one party resists change, it's unfeasible to enforce it without legal action.

Do Prenuptial Agreements Cover Potential Child Support and Child Custody Issues?

Prenuptial agreements can address child support and child custody issues if the child already exists at the time of the agreement. However, if the child is unborn or hypothetical (planned for the future), the enforceability of such provisions is questionable from a legal standpoint.

---

[16] If the proposed change isn't deemed important enough to end the marriage, one should strongly consider going to mediation – rather than retaining an attorney.

Nevertheless, you can include statements of intent in your prenuptial agreement, such as anticipating a joint custody arrangement in case of marital breakdown. However, these provisions are almost always subject to modification based on "changes in circumstances." For instance, if a spouse develops a drug or alcohol problem, or anger management issues that didn't exist at the time of the marriage, these changes may call for reconsideration of the agreed-upon joint custody arrangement.

The key takeaway is that courts are less likely to enforce such provisions unless they're proximate to current circumstances. For instance, if you created your prenuptial agreement just a few months prior to considering divorce, the court might require compelling reasons to not honor your joint custody intent.

Do Both Parties Need to Have An Attorney Present When Signing A Prenuptial Agreement?

While it's important to distinguish between necessity and advisability, it is indeed recommended that both parties have legal representation when signing a prenuptial agreement. This is a legally enforceable contract with potentially significant implications for your future.

If one party, typically the less wealthy, declines legal representation, it is essential to explicitly acknowledge this choice in both written correspondence and in the prenuptial agreement itself. The agreement should clearly state that they have been advised of their right to counsel and are willingly waiving this right.

Additionally, it's crucial to affirm the role of each attorney involved – e.g., "I am not acting as a mediator" - if that's the case. To prevent future attempts to invalidate the agreement based on perceived misrepresentation, it's important to state explicitly in the agreement that the attorney is am representing the interests of one's client, not mediating between the parties (unless, of course, the attorney is acting pursuant to a mediation retainer).

To answer the original question directly: no, it is not legally required for both parties to have an attorney present when signing a prenuptial agreement.

However, much like you'd want legal representation when facing serious criminal charges, it's strongly recommended to (at least) consult with a lawyer before entering into any substantial legal contract, including a prenuptial agreement.

What Happens If One Party Breaches a Prenuptial Agreement?

If one party breaches a prenuptial agreement, it's typically advisable to issue a default notice letter. The parties may also seek marriage counseling or mediation. While a direct conversation may sometimes resolve the issue, formal documentation is necessary if verbal discussions fail. However, this action may suggest that the marriage is beginning to falter, and consulting a divorce or separation attorney might also be advisable.

To enforce the prenuptial agreement, you could potentially sue for breach of contract, though this is rarely pursued. More commonly, the prenuptial agreement is enforced through a legal separation or divorce proceeding.

Settling A Prenuptial Agreement Without Disclosing Assets & Liabilities

Some of my clients have asked me whether they can create a solid prenuptial agreement without disclosing all of their assets and liabilities. The truth is, while it's ultimately up to the parties involved to determine exactly how they want to complete their prenuptial agreement, it is always recommended to be as accurate and detailed as possible. This is especially important if you wish to signify that certain assets should not be considered marital assets. Doing so can ensure they are not shared with the other party in the case of a divorce.

It is best if the two parties either exchange sworn net worth statements - or at least list everything in a "Schedule" that clearly demonstrates each individual's assets and liabilities with their exact value and other significant details[17]. It is very helpful to use

---

[17] A sample Schedule is found in Appendix B at the back of this book.

a "Schedule" to verify the validity of your claims, should that need arise in the future.

The Key Requirements for A Valid Prenuptial Agreement

- A prenuptial agreement must be made in contemplation of a marriage.
- It should contain honest and accurate financial disclosure for both parties.
- Both parties should have a fair opportunity to read over the agreement so they fully understand it.
- Both parties must have adequate opportunity to have the document reviewed by legal counsel, or otherwise waive their right to counsel in writing.
- A prenuptial agreement must be signed by both parties, properly acknowledged[18] and notarized to be legally binding.

---

[18] The document must be executed in the same manner as a deed, which typically involves attaching a certificate of acknowledgment.

Challenging A Prenuptial Agreement After It Has Been Signed & Settled

If one party no longer agrees with the provisions in a prenuptial agreement and wants it vacated, the agreement may be challenged in the context of a separation or divorce proceeding.

Should a prenuptial agreement be challenged after it's signed and settled, the court will consider several factors, such as:

1) Coercion

Any signs of coercion or undue pressure on either party can be grounds for challenging the agreement. Both parties should have access to legal counsel and be able to review the prenuptial without interference or time constraints. Offering the less financially advantaged party the opportunity to consult with an attorney and, if necessary, providing financial support for legal representation can strengthen the agreement's validity.

2) Unfairness

The court may examine whether the agreement is excessively unfair to one party, especially if substantial changes in circumstances have occurred since the agreement was executed.

3) Lack of Disclosure

Proper disclosure of financial information is essential, and failure to provide this information may lead to the agreement being vacated. It's highly advisable for both parties to include detailed and accurate statements of all assets and liabilities. This is the reason for the importance of writing a schedule or net worth statement when drafting the prenuptial.

4) Vagueness

Using vague or poorly defined terms when drafting the agreement increases the likelihood of it being vacated. If any provisions are left vague, it becomes more likely a Judge will be unwilling to enforce them.

While prenuptial agreements in New York offer valuable protection for a person's assets, ensuring their enforceability requires careful consideration and adherence to legal guidelines. No matter what your unique goals may be, the best way to create a truly effective agreement that stands up to legal scrutiny is to consult with a knowledgeable attorney. I always say: "If you have enough assets to protect, then it's worth spending a few thousand on an attorney to protect them."

How Is a Postnuptial Agreement Different From A Prenuptial Or Separation Agreement?

While postnuptial agreements can serve similar functions to prenuptial and separation agreements, they are not the same. Prenuptial agreements are made in anticipation of marriage, while separation agreements typically come into play when parties are physically separated or plan to separate imminently.

Postnuptial agreements can be useful in situations that don't quite fit these molds. For instance, one party might want to protect their assets from potential lawsuits against their spouse, and in such a case, a postnuptial agreement can offer the necessary protection. However, as mentioned earlier, it's critical to ensure these agreements include sufficient "consideration[19]" to be legally binding.

What Issues Can a Postnuptial Agreement Address?

A postnuptial agreement can cover a broad range of topics, mirroring the issues a prenuptial or separation agreement would typically address. These can include matters related to property division, spousal maintenance (or alimony), child support, and even custody/visitation if there's an anticipated physical separation.

Setting custody or visitation arrangements can be complex if there's no imminent physical separation. However, in some cases, parties may agree on such terms while living in separate parts of the same house (or alternating who resides in the house with the kids) –

---

[19] Put simply, this means a "bargained-for exchange."

known as nesting. A postnuptial agreement provides the flexibility to accommodate these arrangements and more, filling the gaps where a prenuptial or separation agreement may not be sufficient.

Are Postnuptial Agreements Enforceable in Court?

As is the case with prenuptial agreements, postnuptial agreements are indeed enforceable in court - provided they meet certain requirements established by the law. For instance, these agreements must have sufficient "consideration," a legal term that implies a mutual exchange of value or rights. This involves each party either providing something to the other party or waiving certain rights.

The agreements must also contain the same required provisions as a prenuptial agreement (thus, see that section above).

The effectiveness of these agreements greatly relies on the expertise of the attorney drafting them. Some may attempt to find cost-effective solutions online, but this often results in poorly drafted agreements which may also fail to meet legal standards for enforceability. In short, if the protection of assets or income is important enough to warrant a postnuptial agreement, it's essential to invest in professional legal counsel to ensure the agreement is enforceable.

How Long Does It Take to Draft A Postnuptial Agreement?

The duration needed to draft a postnuptial agreement varies based on several factors. These may include the need for formal net worth statements, the involvement of attorneys on both sides, and the intricacies of the specific terms needed.

If formal net worth statements are necessitated, this process may take several weeks (or months), as these need to be reviewed & notarized. Further, the agreement drafting process itself may take between two to four weeks, taking into account the caseload and other responsibilities of the attorney's office. This timeframe might extend if there's a need for extensive negotiation around the exact terms of the agreement.

These agreements can range from 20 to 30 pages in length, or even longer if they resemble separation agreements. Nonetheless, it's crucial to remember that a well-drafted, enforceable agreement is worth the wait and effort.

Can A Postnuptial Agreement Be Modified or Revoked After Marriage?

Yes, postnuptial agreements can be modified or revoked. Revocation is simple - destroying the original agreement effectively cancels it, as only the original is generally enforceable under New York State law. Modification, however, requires the same formalities as the original agreement. Both parties must agree to the changes, sign the modified agreement before a notary, and attach a certificate of acknowledgment to it.

Does A Postnuptial Agreement Cover Child Custody and Support?

While postnuptial agreements can address issues such as child custody and visitation, they aren't enforceable by themselves. For example, if one parent violates the agreed-upon custody schedule, the other parent's only remedy is to file a petition in family court or commence divorce proceedings. The postnuptial agreement can then be incorporated into a court order, making it enforceable.

Is An Attorney's Presence Required When Signing a Postnuptial Agreement?

Although not required at the signing stage, it is highly recommended that each party has an attorney during the negotiation and drafting of the agreement. Even if one party chooses not to retain counsel, they should at least be advised to consult with an attorney. The decision to forgo legal advice is ultimately theirs.

CHAPTER 7

LEGAL SEPARATION AGREEMENTS IN NEW YORK

When considering legal separation in New York, it's essential to understand the options, requirements, and implications of your decisions.

The Different Types of Legal Separation

Legal separation can be pursued through two primary avenues:

1) Separation Agreement

The most common and practical method, a separation agreement is a legally binding contract that dictates key aspects of the separation like the division of debts and assets, child custody, visitation, child support, and alimony.

2) Separation Action in Court

The two parties can initiate a "separation action" in court to obtain a judgment of separation. This route is rarely pursued, as it involves lengthy, expensive legal proceedings and is less practical than coming to a separation agreement on your own.

What's Included in A Separation Agreement

A separation agreement in New York is a legally binding contract. It typically addresses the following key issues:

- Property Distribution: This includes houses, co-ops, condos, land, and distribution - or waivers of property assets.

- Financial Matters: Covering bank accounts, investment accounts, retirement accounts, the distribution or waiver of financial assets and debts, and the payment of attorney fees.
- Child Custody & Visitation: Outlining custody arrangements and visitation schedules for all minor children.
- Child Support: Specifying the payment schedule and amount of financial support expected for all minor children.
- Spousal Maintenance (Alimony): Addressing the amount and duration of financial support for a spouse, if applicable.

The Reasons You Might Choose Legal Separation Over Divorce

Legal separation in New York offers couples a viable alternative to divorce, allowing couples to address various issues while preserving certain benefits of marriage. Legal separation can be an attractive option for various reasons:

1) Maintaining Health Insurance: If one spouse relies on the other's health insurance, a divorce could result in the loss of coverage[20]. Legal separation allows for coverage to be continued.
2) Religious Or Moral Reasons: Some couples may not be ready to terminate their marriage for religious or moral reasons. A separation agreement can provide a legal framework for living apart while maintaining the marital status.
3) Time for Reflection: Legal separation offers couples the opportunity to live separately and assess whether divorce is the right decision without immediately ending the marriage.

The Duration of A Separation Agreement

A separation agreement is theoretically indefinite; there is no legal requirement to convert it into a divorce. Many couples do eventually proceed with a divorce, but it's not mandatory. Parties can choose to

[20] A Judgment of Divorce will automatically terminate a spouse's medical insurance coverage, though they may be able to extend coverage via COBRA.

abide by the separation agreement for as long as it suits their needs.

How To Obtain a Legal Separation Agreement In New York

While there are websites offering free or low-cost separation agreements, it's important to realize that these may lack the necessary elements or specificities required for legal enforceability. Having an attorney draft - *or at least review* - your separation agreement ensures it meets all legal requirements and adequately addresses your unique circumstances.

Considering the complexity of separation agreements and their far-reaching implications, seeking professional legal guidance is recommended to obtain a legally sound separation agreement.

Whether you choose legal separation or divorce, it's essential to understand the legal processes involved and consult with experienced legal counsel.

Finally, I refer the reader to the prior sections on divorce agreements, prenuptial agreements and mediation, as many of the insights I shared in those chapters are equally applicable to separation agreements – and thus to preserve brevity, I won't reiterate them here.

That said, separation agreements tend to be more extensive and wide-ranging than mere prenuptial agreements. It's thus even more critical to exchange net worth statements and have full disclosure of incomes and assets. It's rare that a Judge will vacate a properly-drafted & executed separation agreement – and thus important both parties do it right. If done properly, the separation agreement will be incorporated into a Judgment of Divorce – assuming the parties go that route at some point after the separation is signed.

If one is looking to do an agreement without counsel – though not recommended – you may consult the court's website for the format of a separation agreement[21] and well as various worksheets addressing

---

[21] https://www.nycourts.gov/LegacyPDFS/courts/11jd/supreme/civilterm/CH-FORMS/separation_agreement_sample.pdf

maintenance & child support[22] and custody/visitation issues[23] which could be pieced together and incorporated into one full agreement. Nevertheless, you are highly recommended to have the agreement reviewed by a mediator or an attorney prior to executing same.

---

22 https://ww2.nycourts.gov/divorce/MaintenanceChildSupportTools.shtml

23 https://www.nycourts.gov/forms/matrimonial/parenting-plan-form.pdf

Addendum A

AGREEMENT QUESTIONNAIRE

Name of Husband:
Phone No.:
Address:

Name of Wife:
Maiden name:
Phone No.:
Address:

Place of marriage:

Date of marriage:

__prepare Stipulation of Settlement, not Separation Agreement

Plaintiff is __Wife / __Husband

__Defendant in military

__an answer has been filed

Name of Court:

Index/Case No.:

Date of Physical Separation:

CHILDREN -

__no children __1 __2 Number: ___

Name(s), dates of birth and age(s) and whether emancipated of each child:

CHILD CUSTODY -

__Wife to have custody

__Husband to have custody

__joint custody

__but children reside with Wife

__but children reside with Husband

__without residing predominantly with either

__Agreement to be silent on subject?

__recite that upon death of custodial parent, non-custodial parent shall have custody?

__ update other parent w/ change of address?

__ child goes to other parent when parent having child needs to go away (on business/job, etc.)

__ jurisdiction to be NY

__non-custodial parent to have school attendance/access to school recs.

__ notification of illness of child?

__ non-custodial parent to have access to medical records/medical treatment?

__ restrict designations of "Mother" & "Father" to actual Mother & Father?

__ notify other parent when parent having child cannot care for child, needs to go away on vacation, emergency job assignment, etc.

__ refrain from scheduling activities which would interfere with other parent's time w/ child

__ telephone access when child's w/ other parent

__ adoption – both parents must consent

__ failure to exercise not forfeiture

__ mediation in event of disputes

__ restrict religion to current one?

__ Professional Model?

MOVING CHILDREN'S RESIDENCE -

__no restrictions

__visitation rights shall be adjusted

__moving from New York prohibited

__moving more than ____ miles prohibited

__other restrictions:

Restrictions to terminate -

__when children reach majority

__on a specific date:

__remarriage of custodial parent

__health of custodial parent requires move

__Agreement to be silent re termination

VISITATION -

__non-custodial parent to have visitation rights pursuant to a specific schedule

__Sat or Sun weekly vs __ Sat & Sun biweekly (or is it Fri-Sun?)

Specify pick-up/drop-off times or other specifics of the proposed schedule:

__Christian vs __Jewish holidays

How many weeks in summer: [__consecutive]

__non-custodial parent to have "reasonable" visitation

__visitation for non-custodial parent not to be discussed

__"reasonable" visitation rights for grandparents

CHILD SUPPORT -

__non-custodial parent to pay specific amounts for child support for each child -

$ __weekly __biweekly __monthly __other:

__non-custodial parent to pay "reasonable" amounts

__no child support to be sought

__payments increase with Consumer Price Index (CPI)

__payments increase on specific dates - dates and payments:

Re payments for college –

__non-custodial parent to make additional payments while children in college -

$ per per child

__non-custodial parent to pay into a college fund -

$ per per child

__both parties to pay to college fund -

Husband - $ per per child

Wife - $ per per child

__non-custodial parent to pay __all/__one-half of the college expenses [________but not more than $ per annum per child, or ____________cost of attending:

____

__college payments increase with CPI?

Payments to end at the age of __21 __18 __other:

__age if child in college:

__non-custodial parent may claim tax exemptions for children?

__ or alternate exemptions?

MAINTENANCE PAYMENTS TO LESS-MONIED SPOUSE -

__Husband/Wife to pay specific amounts to Wife/Husband?

$_______________ per __weekly __biweekly __monthly __ other:

__Husband to pay "reasonable" amounts

__no maintenance to be provided [__ but less-monied spouse expressly may later apply to a court for maintenance]

__payments to terminate on specific date (other than death/remarriage) – i.e., **duration of maintenance** - date:

__payments increase with CPI

__payments increase on specific dates - specify:

MARITAL RESIDENCE (occupied prior to separation) -

Address:

The marital residence was -

__an apartment

__a __house/__condo/__coop owned by BOTH parties

__a __house/__condo/__coop owned by Husband

__a __house/__condo/__coop owned by Wife

__rented premises (other than an apartment)

Approx. current Market Value:
$______________________________

Property acquired in (specify year):
____

Approx. purchase price of residence:

____

Possession of marital residence to be given to -

__Wife

__Husband

__neither Husband nor Wife -

__marital residence to be sold, rather than used

__marital residence to be sold if party in possession -

__vacates __remarries __cohabits with adult __children emancipated

Legal title to be -

__transferred to Husband and Wife as tenants in common

__transferred to Wife

__transferred to Husband

__left unchanged - __ but sold at a certain triggering point (e.g., youngest reaches 18, 2 years from date of agreement, etc.)

__transferee to pay lump sum for transferor's interest (**buy-out**): $

__transferor to continue to pay expenses of marital residence - describe:

Proceeds of any sale of marital residence to be paid -

__equally by Husband and Wife

__to Wife

__to Husband

__$ to Wife, balance to Husband

__$ to Husband, balance to Wife

__other:

__a minimum acceptable sales price: $

Is marital residence affected by -

__an existing mortgage or similar instrument [Amount: ______________________]

Bank name: ______________________________

__insurance premiums

__real estate taxes

__condo [__coop] charges or fees
To be paid by -

__Husband and Wife in equal shares

__Husband

__Wife

__other:

Minor repairs [__less than $] to be paid by -

__parties equally

__Husband

__Wife

__other:

__Agreement to be silent on subject

__there is **OTHER REAL ESTATE**, the rights to which should be set forth in - describe property and rights:

DEBTS -

__there are marital debts to be listed and paid -

__by Husband -- specify institution & current debt owed:

__by Wife -- specify institution & current debt owed:

__some by Husband and some by Wife -- specify institution & current debt owed:

BANK ACCOUNTS -

__there are accounts containing funds

Approx. amount: $______________________________

To be paid to -

__Husband

__Wife

__Husband and Wife equally

__in some other fashion:

__some accounts have been drained by __Husband / __Wife

__Husband to pay Wife $ to settle claims

__Wife to pay Husband $ to settle claims

__all such claims are waived

__Agreement to be silent on subject

Identify the accounts:

INCOME TAXES -

__parties filed joint returns [__for current year]

__parties are GOING TO file joint returns [__for current year]

Refunds are to be paid to -

__Husband

__Wife

__parties equally

__in proportion to income

__other:

__Agreement to be silent on subject

Any deficiency (or taxes due) are to be paid by -

__Husband

__Wife

__parties equally

__in proportion to income

__party who caused the deficiency

__Agreement to be silent on subject

AUTOMOBILES - **identify autos, who gets them (and any provision re expenses of autos):**

LIFE INSURANCE -

Husband/Wife is to -

__maintain existing insurance

__maintain existing insurance and increase coverage

__procure new insurance (none exists)

__Agreement to be silent on subject

Amount of existing insurance: $

Amount of additional insurance to be procured: $

Total insurance to be maintained: $

The life insurance is to be for the benefit of -

__Wife/Husband, or if she dies children

__just Wife/Husband

__just children

__Wife/Husband to pay portion of insurance premiums - amount or share:

MEDICAL INSURANCE (remember DRL 255 language) -

__Husband/Wife to maintain medical insurance for benefit of -

__Wife/Husband and children [__just minor children]

__just Wife/Husband

__just children [__just minor children]

__Husband/Wife to maintain "major medical" insurance (in addition to basic coverage)

__Husband/Wife need not maintain insurance if Wife's/Husband's employer provides coverage

__requirement for insurance to end on a specific date:

Re the deductible under medical insurance -

__Husband/Wife pays deductible

__s/he pays half the deductible

__s/he pays some other portion:

__Wife/Husband pays deductible

__Agreement to be silent on subject

Should the same rule apply to -

__dental and orthodontic expenses

__all medical expenses not covered by insurance
If not, is anything to be provided:

LAST WILL AND TESTAMENT -

__Parties can freely dispose of his estate

__Husband/Wife must bequeath $______________
to Wife/Husband, or if s/he dies to children

__Husband/Wife must bequeath ___% of his estate to Wife/Husband, or if s/he dies to children

__Husband/Wife must bequeath $_______________
to children directly

__Husband/Wife must bequeath ____% to children

__requirement ends on a specific date:

__Wife/Husband to be subject to same requirement as to his/her estate

__prepare a short form (easier to negotiate)

RETIREMENT PLANS

__Husband/Wife to pay Wife/Husband a portion of a **PENSION PLAN/RETIREMENT**

Company providing plan:

____

Spouse's share - __50% __other: % __ formula based on duration of employment and marriage

List all investment/retirement accounts (who owns, values, etc)

- -

Month in which Agreement will be executed:

____

__other LUMP SUM PAYMENT to be made by __Husband / __ Wife - $

__Agreement to contain representations re NET WORTH and INCOME (both parties recommended to execute net worth statements, or alternatively to set forth itemized schedules as addendum to agreement)

Husband's approx. income: $_________________

Husband's net worth: between $________________ and $_____________________

Wife's approx. income: $_____________________

Wife's net worth: between $_____________ and $____________________

__ Who pays what percentage of counsel fees:

__if there is a material change in economic circumstances, either party may apply to a court for modification

__disputes to be resolved by mediation/arbitration - where:

Prepare -

__Memorandum of Agreement?

__Net Worth Statements?

__a Deed to marital residence?

Addendum B

Schedule

Husband's Income: ___________________________

Husband's Properties:

- Aaa
- Bbb
- Ccc

Husband's Financial Accounts:

- Chase Checking, x1234, $10,624
- Fidelity 401k, x5678, $78,965
- Etc.

Wife's Income: ___________________________

Wife's Properties:

- Aaa
- Bbb
- Ccc

Wife's Financial Accounts:

- Citi Checking, x4321, $10,624
- Janney 401k, x8765, $78,965
- Etc.

About The Author

David Bliven graduated with honors from Syracuse University in 1993 with a B.A. in Sociology. He went on to serve as a statistician with the Office of the Deputy Chief Administrative Judge. He then attended New York Law School where he graduated in 1997 with honors and ranked within the top 15% of his class.

Shortly after graduating, he served as a prosecutor for nearly 3 years with the NYC Administration for Children's Services. While at ACS he prosecuted child support, child abuse & neglect and foster care cases on behalf of the City of New York.

After leaving the prosecutor position, Mr. Bliven opened his present practice in 2000. His practice is currently devoted 100% to Divorce & Family Court cases.

Mr. Bliven has an "AV" rating from Martindale-Hubbell (the highest possible rating in both Legal Ability & Ethical Standards), a perfect 10.0 rating from Avvo ("Superb" rating) and is listed in the "Super Lawyers" directory by Thompson Reuters (a distinction given to less than 5% of all attorneys in each field of practice). He is also a "Certified Financial Litigator" and was honored as a "Super Lawyer" for the NY Metro & Westchester area by *Westchester Magazine* in their October, 2019 issue.

Mr. Bliven has authored the books "Navigating Your New York Divorce Case, "Navigating Your New York Family Court Case," "Navigating Your New York High Net Worth Divorce Case" and "Navigating Your New York Post-Divorce Case." His articles have been published in the New York Law Journal, Nolo.com and Westchester Lawyer Magazine.

TESTIMONIALS

- Anonymous: "During a time, when it seemed as my life was about to fall apart, Mr. Bliven was there to make sure I was protected. Mr. Bliven was there to make sure every "T" was crossed and every "I" was dotted. He made sure I was entitled to my fair share. When children are involved in a divorce, I wanted to make sure they were taken care of for the foreseeable future. Mr. Bliven made it his duty to fight for me when he felt I deserved more retribution. He fought tooth and nail for the needs of my children as well as for me. During a time when things looked bleak, Mr. Bliven made sure my legal and financial needs are taken care of. When beginning this venture, I was scared that I would walk off of this with only my "shirt", but Mr. Bliven made it his job to make sure I was able to resume my life without looking back. I want to thank Mr. Bliven and I would recommend him to anyone who is and is thinking about filing for a divorce."

- Jonathan: "Mr. Bliven came very highly recommended to me by a friend who used to practice family law and had transitioned into other areas of legal practice. I was not disappointed. Mr. Bliven was thoroughly knowledgeable and highly attentive as he helped me smoothly resolve complex child support matters involving international issues of competing jurisdictions. Having had a number of attorneys in the course of my divorce and child custody/support matters over the last 18 years, I believe I am experienced to know that Mr. Bliven is a top family law expert."

- Lou: "Mr. Bliven represented me in a child support case. I was very pleased with the services provided by Mr. Bliven. He is professional, courteous, and knows his stuff! I am completely gratified with the outcome of my case. Thanks to Mr. Bliven's knowledge of family law. Mr. Bliven kept me up to date on all matters pertaining to my case and his billing is fair and accurate for the work he puts into the case. I would certainly recommend him to anyone that is seeking a topnotch lawyer in the area family court."

- Teri Colon: "Although I have not met with Mr. Bliven yet. I contacted his office on a Friday of a Holiday Weekend. His office's response was immediate and I was treated with respect as if I was already a client. His staff took the time to email me immediately and when I called I was given an appointment that accommodates my schedule. Custody matters are very sensitive and clients can be emotional. It was a relief to speak with someone who was not only professional and courtesy, but also showed genuine concern. I look forward to my consultation with Mr. Bliven."

- Ariane: "Mr. Bliven was knowledgeable, informative, and an incredible strategist. He used all of my legal rights to defend me in my case and was extremely professional to work with. I can't thank him enough for his ability to use our rights as law-abiding citizens and to get the job done. David consulted with me on all motions before revealing them to the court or to any other parties. For this I thank him and am grateful for his diligence in representation."

- Gregg: "Although I subscribe to a legal plan through my union (I'm a teacher), I decided to retain Mr. Bliven based on our initial consultation. He seemed much better versed than the less expensive "plan" attorney I spoke to in the child support matter I brought to him. Mr. Bliven scanned the paperwork I brought with me to the consultation and immediately developed a strategy using various points of law. Mr. Bliven kept in constant contact with me and "cc'd" me on all correspondence he and my ex-wife's attorney had via email or hard-copy. Mr. Bliven's courtroom demeanor was just as I had hoped it would be; vocal and on point. Ultimately, my ex-wife and I reached a fair compromise that did not follow the default percentages NY State dictates. I would definitely retain again should the need arise."

- A Satisfied Client: "Navigating family court for personal reasons can be quite intimidating, even for folks who have interfaced with court officers and judges for professional purposes. That said, Bliven was nothing short of extremely knowledgeable, courteous and very attuned with the emotional experience that comes with the process. I highly recommend Bliven if you are seeking consultation and representation with a child support and/or custody case!"

****

More Testimonials may be found on David Bliven's website (http://www.blivenlaw.net/Testimonials.shtml) and at Avvo (https://www.avvo.com/attorneys/10463-ny-david-bliven-952796.html#client_reviews).

* * * *

If you appreciated the information given to you in this book, Mr. Bliven would appreciate a review of the book on Amazon and/or a Google review:

https://g.page/law-offices-of-david-bliven-933/review?rc

INDEX

A

alimony · 11
asset investment accounts · 17

C

certified divorce financial planner · 15
custody or access litigation · 25

D

debt statements · 20
divorce · 9
divorce attorney · 13
Divorce Judge · 24
divorce mediator · 59
divorce process · 23

F

Family Court · 75
Family Court case · 38
financial planner · 16
financial planning · 13

M

marital agreement · 81
marital debts · 17
marital property and wealth · 42
marital residence · 38
Marital Settlement Agreement · 28
Mediation · 83
mediation agreement · 91

N

New York family law · 75

New York State law · 113

P

parent coordinator or facilitator · 59

postnuptial agreement · 81

prenuptial agreement · 81

R

retirement accounts · 17

S

separation agreement · 81

spousal support · 10

NOTES

Made in United States
Orlando, FL
07 November 2026

90339166R00085